Old Knaresborough

Paul Chrystal

The impressive remains of the King's Tower and Porch, originally Norman and rebuilt in 1312 by Edward II. In 1170 the castle was refuge for Hugh de Morville and his accomplices in the slaughter of Thomas Becket. Captured in 1644 by Cromwell in the Civil War it was slighted in 1648. The first Maundy giving, by King John, took place here in 1210.

Knaresborough Castle has its origins in the fortified settlement or *burg*, which was referred to when the Angles named this place *Knarresburg*. Strategically placed on rocks towering over the Nidd some 120 ft below, the fort was developed as a castle by the Normans, traditionally under Serlo de Burgh, who had fought with William at Hastings. In 1130, Henry I authorised Serlo's nephew, Eustace Fitz-John, to develop the castle which soon became a base for hunting wild boar and deer.

In 1205, King John appointed Brian de Lisle and extended and strengthened the Castle until it became one of the most important military and financial centres in the north, a base from which he could control rebellious barons. He authorised the digging-out of a huge dry moat, started in 1204, and the production of quarrels or crossbow bolts in the Castle forges.

King John's castle was completely rebuilt for Piers Gaveston by Edward II between 1307 and 1312, and became a sumptuous residence as well as a stronghold, with a dozen towers and a great keep.

Text © Paul Chrystal, 2023.
First published in the United Kingdom, 2023,
by Stenlake Publishing Ltd.,
54-58 Mill Square,
Catrine, Ayrshire,
KA5 6RD

Telephone: 01290 551122
www.stenlake.co.uk

Printed by P2D,
1 Newlands Road,
Westoning,
MK45 5LD

ISBN 9781840339628

The publishers regret that they cannot supply copies of any pictures featured in this book.

Following his defeat at Bannockburn, Edward II had to contend with troublesome rebellions in England. On 5th October 1317, a rebel knight, John de Lilleburn, took Knaresborough Castle and held it until 29th January 1318, when it was recaptured by the King's forces. Later that year it proved too strong for the Scots to take. From 1328 the Castle became the occasional residence of Edward III and Queen Philippa, including their sons, the Black Prince and John of Gaunt. In 1372, Edward granted the Castle and Honour of Knaresborough to John of Gaunt, Duke of Lancaster, since which time it has been part of the Duchy and therefore belongs to the Queen.

The ruins we see today are of Edward II's castle, reduced to this state in 1648 by Cromwell's Parliamentarians by slighting – the systematic dismantling of Royalist castles. Knaresborough Castle had been taken by the Parliamentarians in December 1644; little remains of its original splendour, except the Barbican Gate, the keep, and the famous panoramic view of the Nidd Gorge which remained impervious to Cromwell's destroying hand.

Introduction

For its modest size Knaresborough has enjoyed, or endured, a disproportionate amount of history. It can also boast an impressive number of influential characters who have left their mark here down the years. Moreover, situated as it is atop a deep gorge above the River Nidd, it offers some breathtaking scenery and elegant architecture which, despite the best efforts of successive council planners, endures today and is one of England's finest townscapes.

Celia Fiennes, that fearless woman who rode side-saddle through England and was the first to visit every county in the land, reached Knaresborough in 1697. On her tour in *Through England on a Side-Saddle* she admired 'the little houses … all built in the rocks', the Crag Chapel, the castle ruins and a 'Cherry Garden with green walkes for the Company to walk in'. Not too much has changed.

After 1066 the victorious Norman barons, including Serlo de Burgh, were allocated various manors. The castle which de Burgh started to build in his manor of Knaresborough would have served as a base when the Normans ferociously put down all English opposition in the Harrying of the North (1070), reputedly not leaving a single village standing between York and Durham. As well as the castle the Normans started building the parish church where some of their architecture still survives, and which was in 1114 owned by Henry I, youngest son of William the Conqueror. The Normans also introduced French which was spoken here by the military, the clergy and officials for another three centuries (Edward III spoke in English at the opening of Parliament, first in 1362). Two principal Norman characteristics were efficient administration and a love of hunting.

Historically speaking we start with the imposing castle constructed by Henry I in 1130 and developed by King John in 1205; its story takes in the refuge it provided for Hugh de Morville and the other murderers of Thomas Becket, its later destruction by Oliver Cromwell and the 800th anniversary celebrations in 2010 of the very first giving of Maundy money by King John which we now know from research undertaken by Arthur Kellett took place in Knaresborough in the castle grounds.

The world famous Chapel of Our Lady of the Crag and the magical, mystical Dropping Well, the second of two magnificent railway viaducts (the first fell down), the zoo and the 'Oldest Chemist Shop in Britain' in the medieval market place are all included here. Mother Shipton – soothsayer and alleged witch – Eugene Aram – schoolteacher, fraudster and murderer – and Blind Jack – musician, smuggler and road builder extraordinaire – populate the book along with the ordinary people of the town as they go about their local trade, industry, socialising and devotions through the years. Then, as now, much of the commerce would take place largely in the bustling ancient market place and the streets leading off it, in the High Street or on the banks of the Nidd. Schools, pubs and the various places of worship – the bedrock of any town – are all shown in their past and present glory.

Knaresborough's economic history includes a range of industries and trades, including leather and shoemaking, the linen industry, rug-making, quarrying, lime kilns, brickworks, clock and watch making, timber merchants, pharmaceuticals, small enterprises manufacturing bottled sauces, lemonade and ginger beer, Baines's butterscotch and other sweets, as well as a burgeoning tourist industry. Liquorice was once grown and sold in Knaresborough, possibly having been introduced by the Trinitarian friars in medieval times. Its abundance in the fields around Knaresborough was noted by Camden towards the end of the 16th century. According to Hargrove, the last of the small enclosures in which liquorice was grown was one on Waterside, whose owner, Simon

Warner, died in 1683. Cherries too had their day, and corn took over by the end of the 18th century making Knaresborough one of Yorkshire's biggest corn markets.

Knaresborough's main industry was linen but this image shows the Knaresborough rug works (Holgates) as painted by Joseph Baker Fountain (1907-1992) with fleeces being washed and drying in the garden; *Pigot & Co. Royal, National and Commercial, 1841* status that the companies based at Low Bridge in the mid 19th century were J Clapham, William Clapham and Co. (both of whom specialised in sheep skin), and William Hartley with Jacob Edmondson in Market Place. Clapham's is next to the gas works in a building which was formerly a soap factory run by Joe Clough.

The trade and craft of cordwaining, the making of boots and shoes, was for centuries an important feature of Knaresborough's economy. There were enough cordwainers in the town to oblige the cobblers in the town to celebrate their patron saint every St. Crispin's Day (25th October), and the *Directory of 1831* listed sixteen boot and shoemakers in Knaresborough, prominent amongst whom was Charles Wox in the 1611 building at 72 High Street. Billie Wox succeeded his father and carried on till his death in 1972. Rope making too was important with a rope works on Crag Top run by the three Johnson brothers and retailed through their shop also on the High Street. Twine was manufactured at Bridge Mill near Low Bridge.

On January 28th 1908 fire ripped through Knaresborough (Sellar's) Leather Works at the junction of Brewerton Street and Union Street. This was not the first time, though: the *Knaresborough Post* of June 24th 1882 reported on 'one of the most alarming and destructive fires that has ever been known in Knaresborough' at the works and warehouses of Mr Henry Stockdale 'spirit merchant, leather cutter and dealer in all kinds of saddlery, harness &c' at the entrance to Park Row… in a marvellously brief space of time the whole building was literally one mass of flame, and presented a most awful and alarming spectacle'.

For most of its early history the population of Knaresborough was small, numbering hundreds and eventually a few thousand, reaching 4,006 by 1821. In this last year the population of High Harrogate by comparison was 1,583 and Low Harrogate 1,010. By

Left: The Rug Works.

the end of the century, however, Harrogate had grown into a town of about 30,000, whereas Knaresborough remained static. By 1911 it had a population of only 5,315, which by 1931 had risen to 5,942. After the Second World War the numbers rapidly increased, rising from 8,950 in 1950 to around 14,000 in 1990. The houses built for commuters to York and Leeds and retirees accounted for much of this increase.

Paul Chrystal, January 2023.

Because Market Place once extended as far as the castle the oldest buildings are on the High Street side with the comparatively recent ones on the south side, one of the earliest of which has a rainwater head inscribed 1741. Nothing remains to show the location of the bull-ring once known to have been here. The stocks, which once held miscreants to be humiliated, are on display in the Courthouse Museum. The most interesting of the attractive buildings are the Oldest Chemist's Shop and the Old Town Hall. From the balcony of the latter, speeches were made during parliamentary elections. The Market Place has been the venue for all kinds of gatherings, as well as the striking of bargains and the hiring of servants The Market Place was once entirely surfaced in cobbles, covered by tarmac in 1963. It was partly pedestrianised in 2002, with a token few cobbles retained round the base of the Market Cross. Few towns can have a Market Cross with as unusual a history as Knaresborough's. The circular stone base dates from 1709, when a new cross was erected. This was replaced in 1824, when the enthusiastic gas engineer, John Malam, donated a gas lamp which can be seen in the earliest photographs. When electricity arrived this was replaced by an ugly bulky transformer and a tall stand, with lamps on three branches.

The 1856 Holy Trinity Church off Gracious Street dominated the horizon with its 166 foot spire; designed by John Fawcett it cost £3,800 to build. Harker's, the rug manufacturers, was at the far end of the bridge; it is now long gone. For hundreds of years before the development of Harrogate, Low Bridge at the bottom of Briggate was the main way into Knaresborough. Originally there was a ford here, then the river was crossed by the Staynbrig (Stone Bridge), also called March Bridge (from an old word for boundary). We don't know when Low Bridge was first built, but there are records of repairs in 1642 and enlargement in 1779. Until about 1908 a cottage near Low Bridge was visited as the birthplace of Mother Shipton. The cave near the Dropping Well, though associated with her from Victorian times, was not publicised as the actual birthplace till about 1918.

The Workhouse – locally known as 't' Grubber'. The first Knaresborough Workhouse was a three-storey whitish building in front of the Parish Church; it opened in 1737 to accommodate about forty paupers. They were looked after by a Master, who was paid £26 15s a year, 'to take care of the Poor finding them Meat, Drink and Fire. Having the Benefit of Work done by the Paupers'. In 1793, the Master, William Borrow, moaned about 'the popularity' of the Workhouse in his report to his superiors: 'Gentlemen, I think they come from all parts of the world to Knaresborough, for they know where they get much made on. Pox take 'em all!' Conditions were shocking, and food wretched – gruel, broth, suet pudding, and little meat. Things got a little better when a new Workhouse opened in Stockwell Road in 1858. A report from the early 20th century shows that 'The County Poor Law Institution, Knaresborough' had a total of 310 residents – '59 infirm men, 36 infirm women, 47 sick males, 66 sick females, 8 maternity cases, 17 children under three, 75 in the casual wards.' Clearly the Workhouse was well down the road to becoming a hospital, and was used as such during the First World War and later adapted as a geriatric unit. Its 1858 architecture was mock Tudor style by Isaac Shutt, architect of the Harrogate Royal Pump Room. Harrogate Borough Council oversaw its demolition in 1996.

Conyngham Hall, Knaresborough.

Coghill Hall, originally Coghill House, a Tudor residence, was built by Marmaduke Coghill in 1555 on the site of an even earlier mansion. The Coghills, who later became connected with the Slingsby family through marriage, included Sir John Coghill, Master of the High Court of Chancery in Ireland, and were for many years landowners, cloth merchants and Royalists. Coghill House was rebuilt as Coghill Hall, the home of Sir John Coghill, then in 1796 restored, enlarged and renamed Conyngham Hall, is based on the old Coghill Hall, which had been rebuilt in the 1760s, probably by John Carr, this was sold, with 51 acres of land along the Nidd, by Sir John Coghill to Ellen, Dowager Countess of Conyngham, hence the name. In 1905, it was bought by the Charlesworth family. Sir Harold Mackintosh, the Toffee King, lived in Conyngham Hall from 1924 to 1942. In 1946, the hall and grounds were bought by the Knaresborough Urban District Council.

Castle Mill stands on the banks of the Nidd just below the castle; it started life as a paper-mill, built in 1770 on the edge of the weir and making use of the water-wheel which had pumped water up into the town since 1764. In 1791 it was rebuilt as a cotton mill, adapted for the spinning of flax and weaving of linen in 1811, and by 1847 had been taken over by the biggest employers in Knaresborough, the firm of John Walton, established in 1785. Walton's were linen manufacturers and a major source of employment in Knaresborough for a century and a half, founded in 1785, and managed by John Walton of Byard's Lodge. By 1838 Walton's employed 272 men, 106 women, 25 boys and 20 girls, the children being educated at Walton's own school. The same year Walton's was appointed suppliers of royal linen by Queen Victoria, with the distinction of being able to weave into their towels names like 'Sandringham' and 'Balmoral'. In 1851, when the firm was well established in Castle Mill, Walton's excelled at the Great Exhibition where they won the Prince Albert Medal. Quality was always maintained, in spite of fluctuations in trade, until the last linen was woven here in 1972.

The manufacture of linen was a cottage industry dating from at least Tudor times. Flax was at first grown locally, then imported from the Baltic via Hull – rising from 500 tons in 1717 to 2,300 tons in 1783. There are many records of Knaresborough people carrying out the processes of retting, boiling, bleaching, heckling, dyeing, spinning and weaving. Writing in 1787 Hargrove says that 'Upwards of one thousand pieces of linen (20 yards by 35 inches) are manufactured in this town and neighbourhood each week.' By 1820 there were twenty-four small firms in the town manufacturing linen, as well as a dozen linen merchants and drapers. The photo shows another of Knaresborough's mills, Abbey Mills. Fulling mills were crucial to Knaresborough's textile industry; fulling, that is, thickening cloth, was carried out in various mills, sometimes known as 'walk-mills', because a 'walker' fulled the cloth by tramping on it. The first known mention of a fulling mill in Knaresborough was as early as 1284. One was built at Spitalcroft in 1525, and apparently survived until 1849, when it was shown on the O.S. map as a 'walk mill'.

Visitors to Knaresborough have been arriving at the town's Grade II listed station since its opening in 1848 on the Harrogate line 17 miles west of York. At the very early date of 1819 a committee was set up to produce *The Report of the Knaresborough Railway*, envisaging what would have been perhaps the earliest line in the country to transport flax, linen, timber, coal, limestone and so on, as well as passengers. Insufficient investment was available so the railway to Knaresborough did not arrive until 30th October 1848. This line from York had to stop at a temporary station at Haya Park because the viaduct across the Nidd collapsed just before being completed in 1848. The following year the tunnel under High Street was finished by George Wilson and his 270 workmen. After the viaduct was rebuilt in 1851 the line extended as far as Starbeck, with a line going through to Harrogate by 1863. Knaresborough Station was completed in 1865, and further developed in 1890. In late Victorian and Edwardian times, and up to the Second World War, hordes of visitors came by train to Knaresborough. The signal box is very unusual in that it was built as an annex onto an existing row of terraced houses at 53 Kirkgate.

To the west of the station is the 300 foot, four span (each 56' 9" wide) viaduct designed by Thomas Grainger Engineering and built by a 270 strong workforce led by George Wilson, railway contractor. It carries the line over the River Nidd 78 feet below. Disaster struck when, nearly complete, it collapsed on March 11th 1848. It took three and a half years to rebuild and eventually opened in 1851 at a cost of £9,803. The picture shows a British Railways inspection taking place in 1960 using the "Gozunda" (hydraulically-operated rail-mounted viaduct inspection unit).

At 12.15 p.m. on Saturday, 11th March 1848, the thunderous roar of falling masonry is said to have lasted five minutes. The foundation stone had been laid amidst great rejoicing the previous April by Joseph Dent of Ribston Hall, High Sheriff of Yorkshire. Poor workmanship, shoddy materials and heavy rain led to it crashing into the river, when almost completed. Tom Collins, later MP for Knaresborough, narrowly missed being crushed, but there was no loss of life, except for multitudes of fish, killed by the lime in the mortar. Waterside was flooded to a depth of 12 ft, and much damage done, but eventually the viaduct was rebuilt to a design by Thomas Grainger at the joint expense of two railway companies. The contractors Duckett and Stead finally completed this spectacular structure, 90 ft high, 338 ft long, with four arches of 56 ft spans – and it was opened on 1st October 1851. Nicklaus Pevsner deplored the way the railway cut through the heart of the town, but J.B. Priestley admired the way the viaduct, reflected in the river, 'added a double beauty to the scene'. William Grainge noted that in 1848, when the viaduct collapsed, locals had started saying that Mother Shipton had always predicted that 't' big brig across t' Nidd should tummle doon twice, an' stand fer ivver when built a third time' – a garbled version of which still survives, linked with the end of the world.

The Nidd has frozen over several times, including 1916, 1929, 1940, 1943 and 1947, with much sliding and skating. Many have drowned in the Nidd, especially in the notorious stretch, Cherry Tree Deep.

Jude O' Brien posted this evocative photo on the *Old photos and the history of Knaresborough* Facebook page, 11th June 2020 with the following caption: 'This is a photo dated 1914 of my grandmother Mabel Young, who lived as a girl in Washington House on Waterbag Bank. She was a champion punter and taught my sister and I. When she was 80 the three of us took a punt each and she challenged us to a race. Guess who won?!'

Just as sedate and even more popular, boating is still a major attraction on the Nidd today. This photo shows Edwardian boaters near the boat houses at High Bridge. The first known provider of boats was William Bluet, who died in 1850. He was followed by Richard Sturdy of Richmond House, whose landing stage and boathouse were just below the castle. The last boat was built here in about 1927. The Nidd has always been essential to Knaresborough's economy – a means of transport, a source of fish, power for the water-wheels of various mills for corn-grinding, fulling, textile manufacture etc., as well as boating. The Nidd also supplemented the wells of the town by supplying drinking-water, though sewage was, until Victorian times, dumped in the river.

The section of the River Nidd running through the town has always been popular for messing about in boats, canoes and punts. Eugene Aram suggested that Nidd is from a word meaning 'below' or 'covered', because it disappears underground in Upper Nidderdale and is a name related to words like 'nether' and to other rivers (e.g. Welsh Nedd and Neder) which are partly underground.

This shows some of the boats built and hired out by Sturdy and Son (140 to Blenkhorn's 90). Founded by Richard Sturdy (1837-1913) about 1850 the firm bought and expanded the boat business previously run by Mr Bluett. Sturdy's built the boats they hired out; this 1914 photo shows Frank Sturdy (son of the founder Richard) at work; Frank did his apprenticeship in York. At this time Frank had taken on George Smith, an apprentice aged 12. To save visitors on Waterside a long walk round to get to the Dropping Well, young George W. Smith, boatman with Sturdy's before the First World War, started his popular 'Penny Ferry', rowing a boatload of up to half a dozen visitors across the river at a penny each. Sturdy's was subsequently taken over by Bill Henry and then sold to Harrogate Council in 1965.

Blenkhorn's boats. By late Victorian times there was an efficient dedicated post office in Knaresborough, run by postmaster Charles Blenkhorn, the boatman and landlord of the World's End. He sold stamps and postal orders, issued licences, took in savings and handled telegrams. His sister was postmistress having previously worked in the Starbeck post office with her father. Long-serving Knaresborough postmen, such as Thomas Thorpe (from 1830) and John Patrick (from 1895) could be delivering letters up to three times a day, and there were three collections from the main pillar boxes in High Street and the Market Place (one on Sundays). We have the names of some of Knaresborough's early postmasters – Stephen Parr, for example, a schoolmaster and trustee of the 1815 Methodist chapel, and Mrs Henrietta Parr, said to have been Britain's first postmistress. The first-known post office was the building at the top of Kirkgate which later became a pork butcher's (Zisler's, then Holch's, now Robinson's).

Launching a boat at Blenkhorn's Boats.

Charles Hubert Blenkhorn, who died in 1966, would often play the part and wear a sailor's outfit. Here he is splicing a rope.

Dick Blenkhorn (on the left) took over from Charles and ran it until he died in 1980.

High Bridge was originally called Danyell Bridge; it was widened in 1773 and then again in 1924 in response to the growing traffic on what is now the A59 Harrogate road. This 1938 picture shows an early traffic policeman, the High Bridge Private Hotel (opened 1906), the New Century Dining Rooms (1900) and the timbered World's End pub in the distance. All three establishments were owned by Charles Blenkhorn who also competed with Richard Sturdy in the boating business.

The Chapel of Our Lady of the Crag or St. Robert's Chapel. This is the correct name for what was for many years mistakenly called 'St. Robert's Chapel', perhaps because it was confused with St. Robert's Cave, also in the rock face, though nearly a mile further down the river. The Chapel was cut out of the crag near Low Bridge by John the Mason in 1408, and is said to be the third oldest wayside shrine in Britain. At 10'6" long, 9' wide and 7'6" high this was "elegantly hollowed out of the solid rock: its roof and altar beautifully adorned with Gothic ornaments " (according to an 1880s official guide to Knaresborough). The entrance is guarded by the figure of a Knight holding a sword, described by early visitors in the eighteenth century as eroded, as is the 19th-century restoration. The Knight is caught "in the act of drawing his sword to defend the place from the violence of rude intruders". Wordsworth visited in 1802, alluding to it in his *Effusion*. Some, including Wordsworth, took this soldier to be one of the Knights Templar. Now officially recognised as a chapel by the Vatican the 1890 second edition of the guide goes on to describe the interior: "Behind the altar is a large niche, where formerly stood an image; and on one side of it a place for the holy water basin. Here also are the figures of three heads designed…for an emblematical allusion to the order of monks (Sanctae Trinitatis) at the once neighbouring priory, by some of whom they were probably cut." A later image of the Madonna and Child is dated from 1916 when the shrine was restored by John Martin. He gave it to Ampleforth Abbey on whose behalf it is now looked after by the parish of St. Mary's, Knaresborough. The current statue was carved by Ian Judd and dedicated in 2000. The Chapel is too small for a congregation, but mass is occasionally said outside.

Born in 1488 (so predating Nostradamus by 15 years) in a cave next to the River Nidd, the legendary Mother Shipton (née Ursula Southeil) is synonymous with Knaresborough and with the art of prophecy. Afflicted by what was probably scoliosis and variously branded a witch and the devil's daughter her predictions have included the demise of Cardinal Wolsey, the Gunpowder Plot, the Great Fire of London, her own death, and, as yet unsuccessfully, the end of the world (1881 and 1991)! In 1667, a fictionalised account of her by Richard Head stated she had been born (after her mother had been seduced by the Devil in disguise) at Knaresborough, 'near the Dropping Well'. Head's publication contains the first of many fabricated prophecies attributed to Mother Shipton, all written *after* the events (e.g. the defeat of the Spanish Armada). Forgeries were taken a stage further by the unscrupulous Brighton bookseller, Charles Hindley, who in 1873 confessed that he had made up prophecies about modern inventions and one that had caused much alarm: 'Then the world to an end shall come In eighteen hundred and eighty one'.

Evidence of belief in witches is the font-cover, once locked into place to prevent holy water from being stolen. An example of such theft is the case of a Knaresborough schoolmaster, John Steward, who in 1510 was arrested and accused by an ecclesiastical court in York of stealing holy water and using it to baptise a cockerel, cat and other creatures and of conspiring to seek buried treasure by means of witchcraft. No other individuals in Knaresborough are recorded as suspected witches, and Mother Shipton, in spite of Wolsey's threat to have her burnt, and later fiction by Richard Head, has nearly always been presented as a prophetess, rather than a conventional witch. The Oldest Chemist's Shop sold quills of quicksilver (mercury) to be carried on the person to ward off evil spirits, but this was in the 1700s, and such superstitions have, in general, long since disappeared.

One of Britain's oldest tourist attractions, the Dropping Well derives its name from the water dripping over a limestone rock into a little pool, before joining the Nidd. The earliest known description is by John Leland, the antiquary of Henry VIII. After his visit in about 1538 he wrote of 'a Welle of a wonderful nature, caullid Droping Welle. For out of the great rokkes by it distillith water continually into it… what thing so ever ys caste in and is touched of this water, growth ynto stone.' A tourist attraction since 1630 the Petrifying Well has intrigued visitors with its seemingly magical ability to change everyday objects into stone by depositing layers of calcite. Seven hundred gallons of water flow through every hour and it takes approximately six months to "petrify" a teddy bear, for example. The overhang is nowadays regularly scraped to prevent collapse, as happened in 1704, 1816 and 1823. Neither Leland nor any other early visitor refer to a nearby cave, later claimed to be the birthplace of the Tudor prophetess, Mother Shipton, though the two are now closely associated.

The Dropping Well Inn, also known as Mother Shipton's Inn. The Dropping Well estate was run by a Mrs Comer and her five daughters in the early 20th century until they were forced to leave when the Slingsby family lost the Slingsby baby case (concerning the legitimacy of their child and its right to the family's fortune) in 1916. The inn was close to the local gibbet on which the notorious Eugene Aram rotted away. Born at Ramsgill in Nidderdale in 1704, Aram moved to Knaresborough in 1734 and opened a school at the top of High Street in White Horse Yard (now Park Square). A self-educated scholar and linguist, he became involved in a fraudulent scheme with a flax-dresser, Richard Houseman, and a young shoemaker, Daniel Clark. On 7th February 1744, Clark disappeared, and it was assumed he had absconded with the defrauded valuables. Soon afterwards, Aram paid off his debts and left Knaresborough. In August 1758, a skeleton was discovered, buried on Thistle Hill. Houseman, accused of Clark's murder, denied that the bones were Clark's and eventually confessed that he was buried in St. Robert's Cave where he had seen Aram strike Clark down. Traced to King's Lynn, the schoolmaster was arrested and imprisoned in York Castle. In spite of his learned defence speech he was found guilty at York Assizes and, on 6th August 1759, condemned to be hanged in York, and later hung on the gibbet in Knaresborough, just above the Mother Shipton Inn. Two writers made Eugene Aram well known to Victorians – Thomas Hood in a *The Dream of Eugene Aram* vividly describes his guilty conscience, and Bulwer Lytton in a fanciful novel, *Eugene Aram*, which attempts to exonerate him. The inn was part of the Slingsby estate. Sir Charles Slingsby was perhaps the most famous member of the family; he died tragically on a ferry on the River Ure at Newby Hall while out hunting in 1869 along with 6 other men and eight horses. His sister, Emma Louisa, dedicated a tomb to Sir Charles in the Slingsby Chapel in the parish church of St. John the Baptist.

First World War wounded or recuperating officers en route to one of the local military hospitals stopping off for a pint at the Dropping Well. The truck was operated by Smith's Jams of Shipley; note the dogs. The soldiers were probably destined for Knaresborough Auxiliary Military Hospital in the old workhouse building on Stockwell Road. The hospital opened in November 1916 with 47 beds and was run by West riding 42 VAD. The first Commandant was Lady Evelyn Collins. It closed in November 1919 having treated 573 patients and became the site for Knaresborough Hospital which was demolished in 1996.

The *Marigold* houseboat (along with the Moat Cafe) was owned for most of its life by the O'Reilly sisters, who also ran the Moat Café; it housed a stylish restaurant, serving food on the upper deck and played a key role in the annual Water Carnivals as the venue for a brass band; unfortunately it sank in 1920. Sometimes the *Marigold* sailed on the river. The riverside Marigold Café preserves the old name.

A pensive lady on *Marigold*.

The Hut in Long Walk, the riverside avenue offering fine views of the town, which leads from High Bridge to the Dropping Well. This was much used in the days when 'Knaresborough Spa' still referred to the town itself, and later when Harrogate had taken over as *the* spa, and visitors came to Knaresborough for recreation as part of 'the cure'. Daniel Defoe records walking along here in 1717. The Long Walk was later landscaped by Sir Henry Slingsby in about 1739. It was used by Madame Doreen – palmist and clairvoyant – who gave special consultations, by appointment.

The World's End pub on High Bridge dates from around 1898 when it replaced the original tavern there. It was owned by Charles Blenkhorn.

A photograph from the early 1900s showing the wood-paneled Old Oak room inside the Crown Hotel with a customer enjoying a quiet read; the only thing missing is a pint of ale. *Baines Directory 1822* lists 39 other pubs and hotels in Knaresborough. Around this time the Crown boasted an impressive external clock, was owned by Tetley's and the landlord was a W. Broadley.

This 1969 photo shows Knaresborough Zoo's owner Edward Milborrow with Irma the elephant. The zoo was established in the grounds of Conyngham Hall in 1965 under Nick Nyoka, who made expeditions to the world's jungles to bring back exotic animals. These included Simba, at the time the biggest lion in captivity. The zoo became popular with tourists, drawn especially to Nyoka's snake-handling dremonstrations. (*Nyoka* is Swahili for 'snake'.) Irma the elephant was something of a film star and shared her home with breeding bears, lions, tigers, llamas, wallabies, penguins and monkeys. In its heyday the zoo attracted 150,000 visitors each year, 10,000 of these in school parties. However, by 1985 conditions were not considered satisfactory by Harrogate Borough Council, who refused to renew the licence. A campaign to close the Zoo was supported by a visit from Virginia McKenna; others pleaded for its retention, but there was no financial backing, and after an unsuccessful appeal, it closed in November 1986. Much of the zoo's land was developed by Henshaw's Art and Craft Centre in 1999.

Nick Nyoka, the Stockton-born zookeeper and owner, was described in the *Daily Telegraph* as a fearless subjugator of wild animals. He owned 'Cassius' which, at 28ft. was the longest snake in captivity and also 'Simba' the largest captive lion in the world which he caught on the Serengeti Plain in 1959. The lion weighed 826 lbs and consumed more than 20 lbs of meat and a gallon of milk every day. It appeared in the film *Cleopatra* with Elizabeth Taylor in 1963.

Blind Jack is the nickname of John Metcalf, who was born in 1717 in a cottage (demolished in about 1768) near the Parish Church and was a true Jack of all trades. He went to school at four, but at the age of six was afflicted by smallpox, which left him completely blind. An intelligent lad with prodigious determination and energy, he led an active life tree-climbing, swimming, hunting and gambling. At the age of 15 he was appointed fiddler at the Queen's Head in High Harrogate. Later he earned money as a guide (especially at night-time), eloped with Dolly Benson, daughter of the landlord of the Royal Oak (later the Granby), and in 1745 marched as a musician to Scotland, leading Captain Thornton's 'Yorkshire Blues' to fight Bonnie Prince Charlie's rebels.

Blind Jack is best known for his work as a pioneer of road-building. His extensive travels and the stage-coach he ran between York and Knaresborough had acquainted him with the appalling state of English roads. Soon after a new Turnpike Act was passed in 1752 he obtained a contract for building (with his gang of workmen) a three-mile stretch of road between Ferrensby and Minskip. Then he built part of the road from Knaresborough to Harrogate, including a bridge over the Star Beck, and went on to complete around 180 miles of road in Yorkshire, Lancashire and Derbyshire. The specially-constructed via-meter he used to measure his roads can be seen in Knaresborough's Courthouse Museum.

Following Dolly's death in 1778 he went to live with one of his married daughters in Spofforth. Here, after many active years in business and as a violin-player, he died in 1810, leaving behind four children, twenty grandchildren and ninety great and great-great grandchildren. A tombstone in Spofforth churchyard pays tribute to the remarkable achievements of 'Blind Jack of Knaresborough'.

This emotive photograph was taken just before the Second World War by C. A. Brotherton and entitled "Down and Out" – a stark reminder of the poverty which existed in Knaresborough at the time. Local legend Blind Jack (really John Metcalf 1717-1810) now occupies a bench nearby, impressively cast in bronze by local artist Barbara Asquith in February 2009.

Firing the Royal Salute. This 24-pounder muzzle loader canon was captured at Sebastopol during the Crimean War and presented to Knaresborough in 1857. Originally it was kept in a railed enclosure in the Castle Grounds, near the War Memorial. On special occasions, or for a small fee paid to Charles Coates, harmless lumps of turf were fired across the gorge. The cannon and its railings were taken away for salvage during the Second World War. A few yards to the left of the War Memorial this photo shows a salute being fired to mark the Coronation of George V in June 1911.

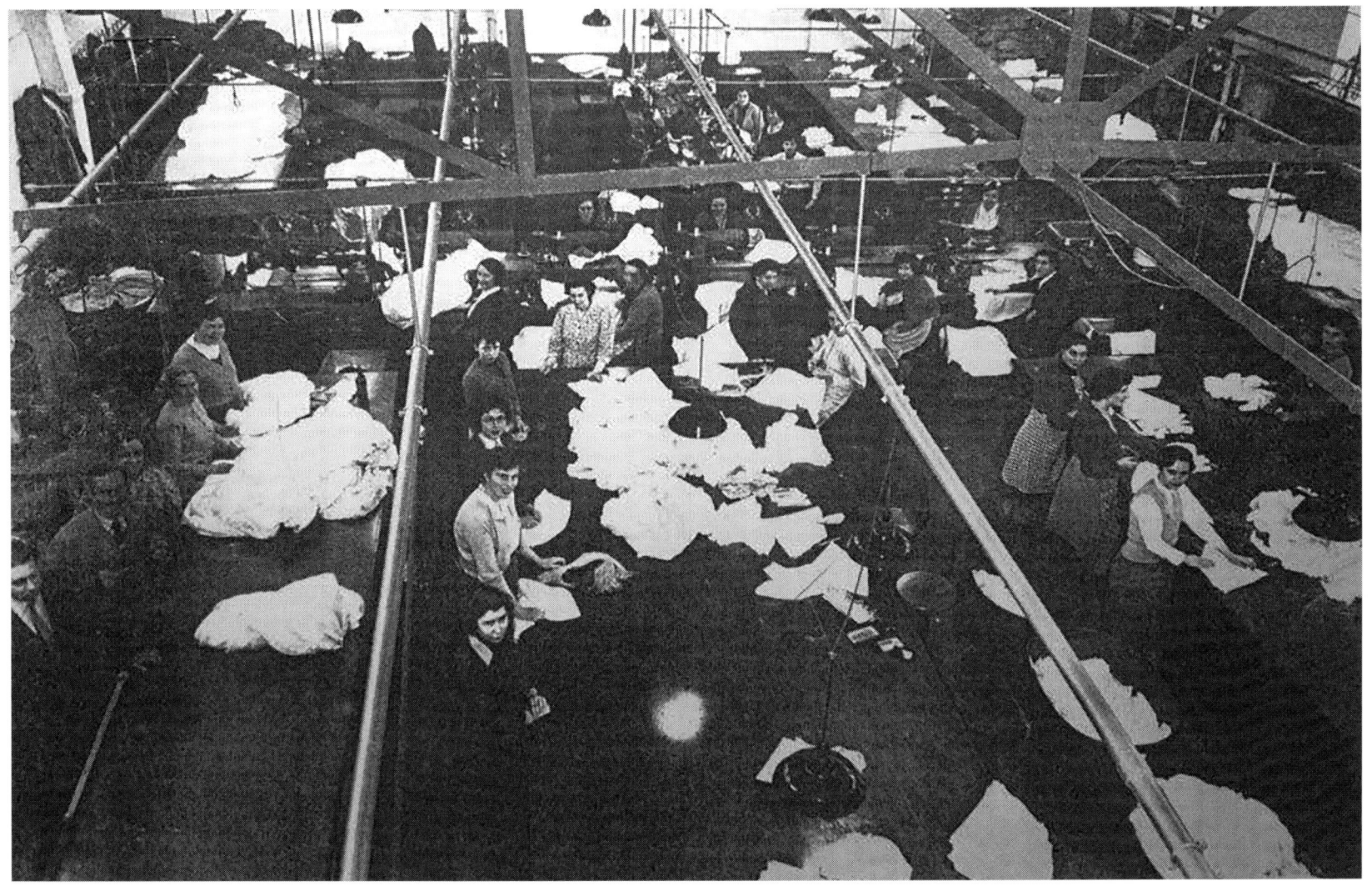

The parachute factory in Isles Lane around 1956. Posted by Leisa Tweedy on the *Old photos and the history of Knaresborough* Facebook page. Sylvia Tweedy, Leisa's mother is on the left hand bench at the back.

One of the annual Tradesmen's Processions which took place every June before the First World War. Here we see the 1909 event and the float from Pickersgill's, the High Street grocers. Horncastle's cycle shop is on the left with the Castle café on the horizon.

"England's Unique Water Pageant". A magnificent spectacle which really came to life after nightfall when Brock's provided a fantastic firework display. The viaduct was transformed into Niagara Falls. A fairy castle, the Eiffel Tower, the houseboat (*The Marigold*) with 40 dancers; a procession of flower-bedecked boats led by the 'Fairy Queen of the Carnival', with more music, including mandolin bands, pierrots and glee choirs on floating platforms of punts or boats tied together, and the backcloth of a fairy palace and dancers on the far bank in the Dropping Well estate. Then there was the brass band, and a spotlight picking out notable local characters such as Mother Shipton to complete the scene.

We don't know when the first Water Carnival was held but it was at its heyday in late Victorian and Edwardian mid-summers when great crowds filled the seats, specially constructed by Kitching's, below the castle, with a perfect view of Sturdy's boat-landing and the river. An idea of the spectacular entertainment is given by the surviving coloured postcards and programmes. Best remembered was the daring tightrope stunt of Don Pedro, perilously pushing a man across the Nidd Gorge in a wheelbarrow, and the Water Carnival at night, with illuminated boats, myriads of coloured fairy-lights set up by George Smith.

There was a Water Carnival in 1913, with huge crowds and receipts of £560, but with the First World War the tradition lapsed, until it was revived after the Second War and held throughout the 1950s.

King James's Grammar School had been founded in 1616 by permission of the King on the instigation of the Rev Dr Robert Chaloner; he was "to take paines with all indifferently, as well poore as rich." Anyone "unapte to learne" after a year was expelled. Zero tolerance too on absenteeism: "he shall be utterly expelled" – unless caused by illness. The original school rules (Ordinances and Lawes) dictated that discipline be enforced by "a rod, moderately": "The Maister…shall severely punish swearing, lying, picking, stealing, fighting and quarrelling, wanton speech and unclean behaviour." In the early days school started at 6.00am in the summer, 7.00am in the winter with an assembly in which the boys recited, on their knees, not just any old Psalm but the longest of them all: *Psalm 119* (176 verses); the Creed, the Lord's Prayer and the Catechism. After year 1 they had to converse in Latin at all times including playtime. Parents were responsible for the provision of bows and arrows (for practice, in case of war) as well as books and all writing materials, and candles in winter. The photo shows, by comparison, a very normal woodwork class in 1952.

Early references to Knaresborough's weekly cattle market show that it was held in the High Street, and that the obstruction, muck and stench were a constant nuisance. In Victorian times the Improvement Commissioners ordered the washing-down of the filthy street after each market day, but it was not until 1907 that a permanent site for the cattle market was established on land between High Street and Stockwell Road.

The geese were not much better – what with the honking and the clatter of their booted feet – worn to make the journey to market more comfortable.

The Priory of St. Robert of Knaresborough, never officially an 'abbey', was founded soon after the Saint's death (1218) by the Trinitarian friars. Following the example of St. Robert, they went round collecting alms, recognised by their white robes which were marked by a distinctive cross of a red upright and a blue cross-bar. They divided the money into three parts: the first was for the upkeep of the Priory, the second for the poor of Knaresborough, and the third for paying the ransom of prisoners taken by the Saracens during the Crusades. Their rules forbade them to ride on horses (though donkeys were acceptable) or to enter taverns. Their first known Charter was granted in 1257 by King John's youngest son, Richard, Earl of Cornwall and Lord of Knaresborough. The site of the Priory was on the misnamed Abbey Road, near the river, on land roughly between the houses known as 'The Abbey' and 'The Priory', the latter having fragments of the original Priory built into its garden wall and the gable end of an outbuilding. A coloured stained-glass window showing the Priory gate-house can be seen in Pannal Church, founded in 1343 by John Brown, one of 'the brethren of the House of St. Robert'. In 1538, the Priory was suppressed on the orders of Henry VIII. It was the only branch of the Trinitarians in Yorkshire.

Built into the crag overlooking Low Bridge, the unique House on the Rock was excavated and constructed by an impoverished (and eccentric) weaver, Thomas Hill, and his son between 1770 and 1791. They also terraced the adjacent land and made a tea garden. The house was then finished off with battlements, and named Fort Montague in honour of the Duchess of Buccleugh, who was its principal benefactress. The son, who had sixteen children, now styled himself 'Sir Thomas Hill', flew a Union Jack from the battlements, fired salutes from a two-pounder cannon and printed his own banknotes – 100,000 estimated to have been in circulation by 1812, but only promising to pay '5 half-pence'. Sometimes also called 'The Swallow's Nest', this became 'The House in the Rock' in the 1930s. For 200 years it was a popular tourist spot, with visitors in more recent years shown round the house by Miss Hemshall and her niece, Nancy Buckle. In 1994, it was closed by Harrogate Borough Council, partly for safety reasons, but in spite of international media interest in the campaign generated by Nancy Buckle and her supporters to keep it in the public domain, the house was put on the market by Ampleforth Abbey in 1997, and has been a private residence since 2000.

Knaresborough Spa Baths

Knaresborough Spa was at Starbeck, on land which had been included in the boundary of Knaresborough by the 1778 Enclosure Act. The revival of an earlier spa here was promoted mainly through Knaresborough chemist Michael Calvert and Dr Peter Murray. A public meeting was held in Knaresborough Town Hall in March 1822, forming a trust with a hundred shares, and two months later the foundation stone of a new Pump Room was laid by the 'Masons of England' following a procession from the Elephant and Castle, High Street. By 1828 a suite of baths had been added for both warm and cold bathing. It was claimed of those who regularly drank the spa water – both sulphur and chalybeate – that 'the digestion becomes amended, the bowels and kidneys perform their functions in a more regular manner… and the skin itself gradually assumes a natural and healthy state'. Knaresborough Spa never managed to rival the well-established mineral wells of High and Low Harrogate, with their superior accommodation and posh visitors, and by about 1890 it had closed down. Some of the early buildings can still be seen near the Star Beck, on Spa Lane, including the later Prince of Wales Baths (1870). The term 'Knaresborough Spa' had also been used to describe Knaresborough itself in the 17th. As well as Starbeck, there was also the Dropping Well, and St. Robert's Well, and St. Mungo's Well at Copgrove. Long after the term 'Knaresborough Spa' had fallen into disuse it was applied to the renewed development at Starbeck.

A pharmacy at least from as early as 1720, when John Beckwith was the apothecary. The inventory of an earlier Knaresborough apothecary, Ralph Metcalfe, shows that in 1689 he stocked as many as 280 different herbs, oils, unguents and chemical powders for his medicines and remedies. Later the Lawrence family ran what was named the Oldest Chemist's Shop. As father and son, William Pierpoint Lawrence and Edmund Lawrence sold everything from corn cures to sheep dip for almost a hundred years, Edmund retiring in 1965, but active well into his nineties. Until 2003 the shop retained many of the original features, including the box-windows on legs of 'Chinese Chippendale' (added about 1760), oak-beamed ceiling, old drawers and coloured bottles, bleeding couch, leech jar, huge pestle and mortar (turned by a dog), pill-making machine, and a small rack which once held quills of quicksilver, worn to keep both diseases and witches away.

Pickles Ointments was a 'pharmaceutical' firm brought to Knaresborough in 1967 by Stanley Horner. In 1994, Pickles bought the Oldest Chemist's Shop, whose tradition of making ointments chimed well with its own successful products, such as 'Snowfire' and 'Fiery Jack'. The Oldest Chemist's Shop ceased to trade as a pharmacy in 1997.

Old English Lavender Water was originally made to a secret recipe by the Lawrence family, who sold it for many years in their shop. One of the most popular Knaresborough souvenirs was the old-style bottle of lavender water, 'mellowed by age and of rare and subtle fragrance', encased in wicker and bearing a red seal stamped with the date of the shop's origin, 1720.

Water Bag Bank falls steeply at the lower end of Kirkgate, where it descends to the Nidd, the only fully cobbled street in the town. Its name arises from the fact that leather bags of water were for centuries carried up here from the river, usually slung across the backs of donkeys and horses. In addition, women – just like Jack and Jill – carried pails of water up the hill, at a half-penny a time. Manor Cottage, a Tudor building at the bottom of Water Bag Bank, is one of the oldest and most pleasing houses in Knaresborough, and the only one to have retained its thatched roof. Lord Philip Inman was born in 1892 in this lowly thatched cottage – his was a classic rags to riches story. Philip's first job was as a paper-boy for Parr's, then a bottle-washer and errand-boy for the Oldest Chemist's Shop. With the background of the parish church, where he was a choirboy, then encouraged by fellow Methodists, he eventually got a job in 1921 as Secretary of Charing Cross Hospital, proving himself to be an enterprising and energetic fund-raiser. For 58 years he served as Secretary, then Chairman, then Life President. Other work included being Chairman of the BBC, the Tourist Board and British Rail Catering. In 1946, he was raised to the peerage for distinguished public service and in 1947, was created Lord Privy Seal, taking as his title Lord Inman of Knaresborough, and calling his Sussex home 'Knaresborough House'. He died in 1979, aged eighty-seven. The site of his birthplace in Water Bag Bank (to the right here) is marked by a plaque unveiled by Lady Inman in 1981.

Old Manor House gets its name from the old Manor of Beechill, though it stands just outside this, and according to W.A. Atkinson, it was not the actual Beechill Manor House which stood opposite the parish church. It is of great age, being built round an ancient roof-tree, now concealed in a cupboard, and with a chequered exterior, shown in early photographs, which may have influenced other black-and-white features in the town. Two stories about the Old Manor House have no historical foundation whatsoever. First, that it was supposed to be a hunting-lodge used by King John. Second, that 'Cromwell slept here' and – according to the novelist Halliwell Sutcliffe – even signed a treaty here with Charles I. Atkinson rightly argued that the Cromwell story came from the fact that the bed in which he slept (at the house in High Street) was moved here and placed in the beautifully-panelled Cromwell Room. From the 17th century the Old Manor House was owned by the Roundell family for nearly 400 years. It was popular as a riverside café, but is now a residence.

Sharon Wylie posted 'My grandparents' [James Mason's] sheepskin factory on Waterside on the 'Old photos and the history of Knaresborough' website, 20th April, 2020. James Mason emigrated to New Zealand in 1951.

From Pauline Mason – James Mason on the left, Harry Mason (?), his son and Pauline's father on the right.